IN THE BEGINNING

A Humorous Survey of the Bible

Written by Helen Reichert Lambin
With Drawings by ISZ
And a Foreword by Rev. William Burke

ACTA Publications
Chicago, Illinois

IN THE BEGINNING
A HUMOROUS SURVEY OF THE BIBLE

Written by Helen Reichert Lambin
With Drawings by ISZ
And a Foreword by Rev. William Burke

Editing by Sr. Rita Benz, BVM
Design by John Dylong
Typesetting by LINK Book Development and Production

Copyright © 1991 by ACTA Publications
4848 N. Clark Street
Chicago, IL 60640
312-271-1030

All rights reserved. No part of this publication may be reproduced by any means without the written permission of the publisher.
Printed in the United States of America

Printing: 6 5 4 3 2 1
Year: 1996 95 94 93 92 91
Library of Congress Catalogue Card Number: 91-073235
ISBN: 0-87946-058-X

To Fr. Gerry Weber

He who laughs last, laughs best.

CONTENTS

Foreword by Rev. William Burke 7

A is for Adam 12
B is for Balaam 14
C is for Corinthians 16
D is for Deborah 18
E is for Elizabeth 20
F is for Felix 22
G is for Goliath 24
H is for Herods 26
I is for Ishmael 28
J is for Jacob 30
K is for Kings 32
L is for Leah 34
M is for Moses 36
N is for Nehemiah 38
O is for Oreb 40
P is for Phoebe 42
Q is for Quelle 44
R is for Rebekah 46

S is for Saul 48
T is for Titus 50
U is for Uriah 52
V is for Vatican 54
W is for Women 56
X is for Xerxes 58
Y is for Yahweh 60
Z is for Zachary 62

About the Humorists 64

Foreword

One of my earliest memories is of the wedding picture of my father's parents. The old photo sat on my aunt's table at precisely my three-year-old level, and my eyes drank in the dignified gentleman with the mustache, sitting in a massive chair, the earnest young woman behind him, hand on his shoulder.

My grandfather was already dead when I was gazing at his younger self, but my grandmother was alive and—well—larger than life. Heroic. I worshiped her. She had come from Ireland at age 16 in a wretched liner, lived at first with friends and relatives, and in hard days had worked hard hours to make her place in America. And, of course, because of her accomplishment, my family had been able to grow and prosper. She was our matriarch, an icon before I knew what the word meant.

When *I* was 16—all eagerness and armed with a tape recorder—I interviewed my grandmother for a school assignment. I asked her why she had left home those many years ago and if she'd ever go back to Ireland (myself, you see, perishing to go there). I waited for an epic answer that would make my report a classic, a sociological *tour de force.*

She looked at me with a sober face and said, "When I rode in the johnny cart to the boat, it rained all over my best dress. So I'm never goin' back."

I stared at her, then laughed out loud. "Seriously, Gram," I said. But she was silent, her eyes regarding me with amusement, as if to say "make of that what you will."

So was my iconic, epic account of my family origin reduced to a johnny cart and a wet dress. (Symbols, I now see, of a poverty unmourned for.)

For all of us, there must be those moments when we look into Scripture and experience the same shock: that God works in human ways, and with human beings, and the events of sacred history seem equal parts absurdity and epiphany. "God's folly," Paul wrote, "is wiser than our wisdom," and probably added under his breath, "Thank goodness!"

In this charming little book, Helen Lambin and ISZ help us look at familiar—and, unfortunately, sometimes not so familiar—people and ideas from the Bible with a humorous eye, and so afford us the shock of the human. They work in the tradition of Jonah's whale and Balaam's ass, of Sarah's sarcasm and Moses' frustration: "What am I to do with these people?"

What indeed? God's love endures with our foibles and weaknesses, and there precisely is where the Divine Pity shines through.

Enjoy this book! And make of it what you will.

Rev. William Burke

"In the beginning
was the WORD..."
John 1:1

A is for ADAM,
who weathered the Fall—
Peking, Cro-Magnon
or Neanderthal?

See Gen 1-3

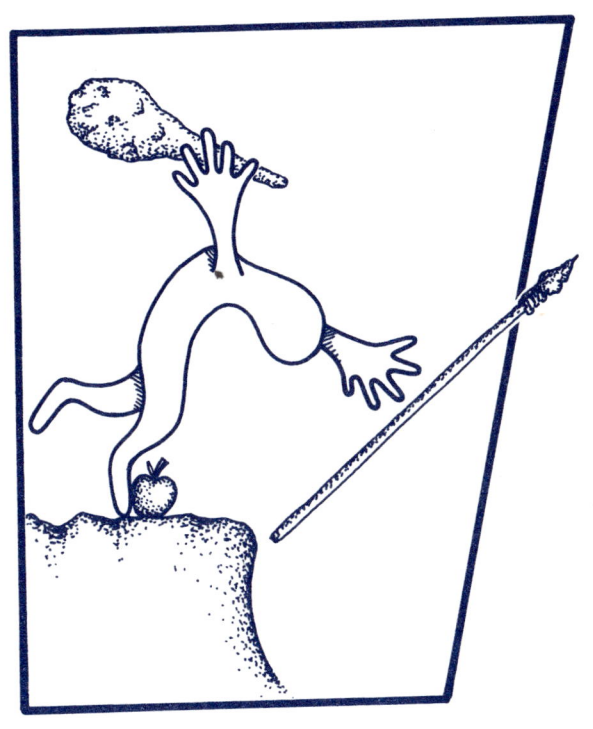

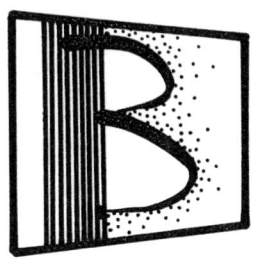

B is for BALAAM,
made wise by an ass
when his spy operation
had reached an impasse.

See Num 22:1-35

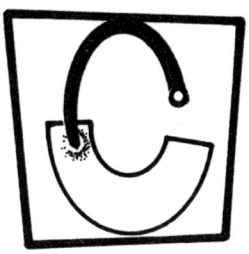

C is for CORINTHIANS,
some lamentably lewd.
Others formed factions,
became drunks, or sued.

See 1 Cor 3:3-9, 5:1-2,
6:1-8, 11:17-22

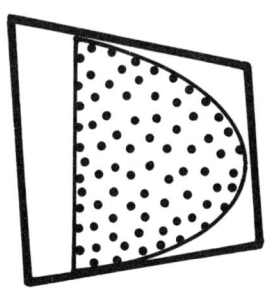

D is for DEBORAH,
a judge most infusive.
Her gift of charisma
was gender inclusive.

See Judg 4-5

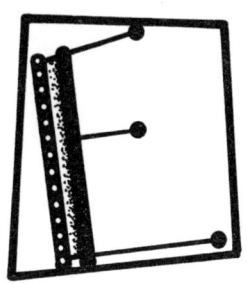

E is for ELIZABETH,
John's mother foretold,
who showed baby boomers
you're never too old.

See Lk 1:5-80

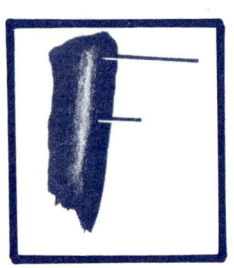

F is for FELIX,
who wanted to talk
but expected a bribe
to let St. Paul walk.

See Acts 24:22-27

G is for GOLIATH,
o'er-boastful, o'er-grown.
Bashed in the head
by a kid with a stone.

See 1 Sam 17:1-54

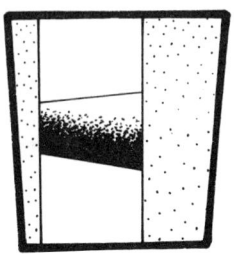

H is for HERODS,
the Great and the Fox.
If they hadn't been kings,
they'd have been behind locks.

> *See Mt 2:1-18; Mk 6:14-29;*
> *Lk 1:5, 13:31-32, 23:6-12*

I is for ISHMAEL,
   whom Abraham sired.
It was Sarah's idea,
but Hagar was fired.

See Gen 16, 21:1-21

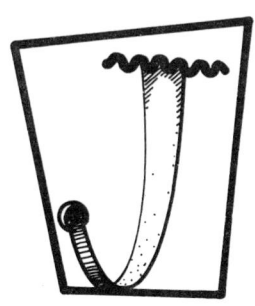

J is for JACOB,
unbrotherly schemer,
wrestler, con-artist,
tither and dreamer.

See Gen 25:19-34; Gen 27-28

K is for KINGS,
who were often egregious.
The prophets were better,
and much more prestigious.

See 1 and 2 Kings

L is for LEAH,
fair Rachel's plain sister.
Only by darkness
would Jacob have kissed her.

See Gen 29:9-35

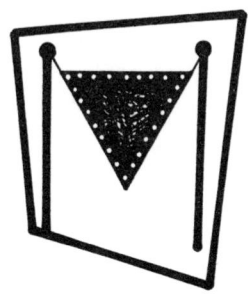

M is for MOSES,
Sinai's law-giving son.
Broke all ten commandments
without breaking one.

See Ex 32:1-20

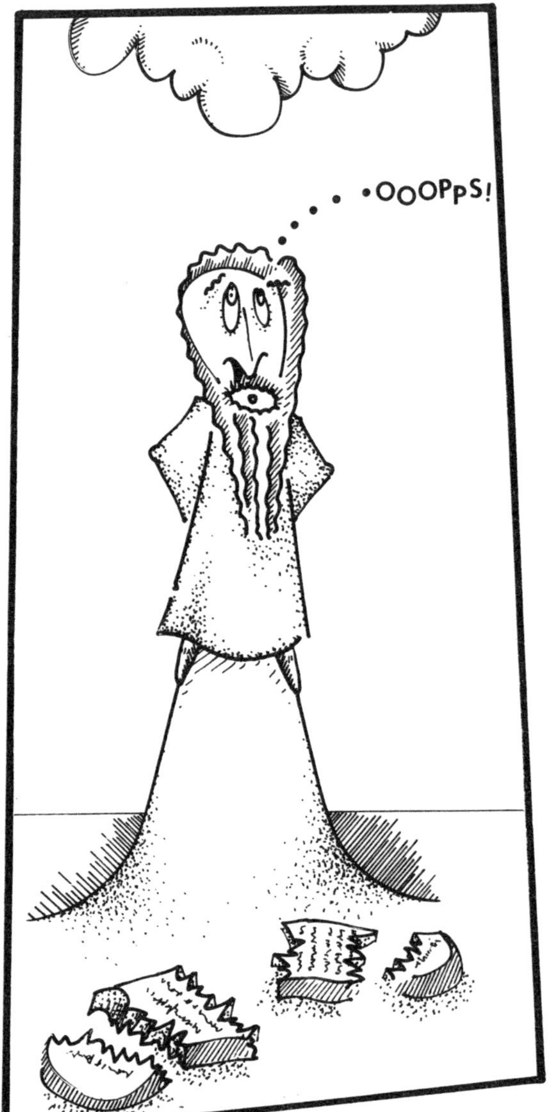
OOOPPS!

N is for NEHEMIAH,
who sent foreign wives home.
No one knows if
he had one of his own.

See Neh 13:23-31

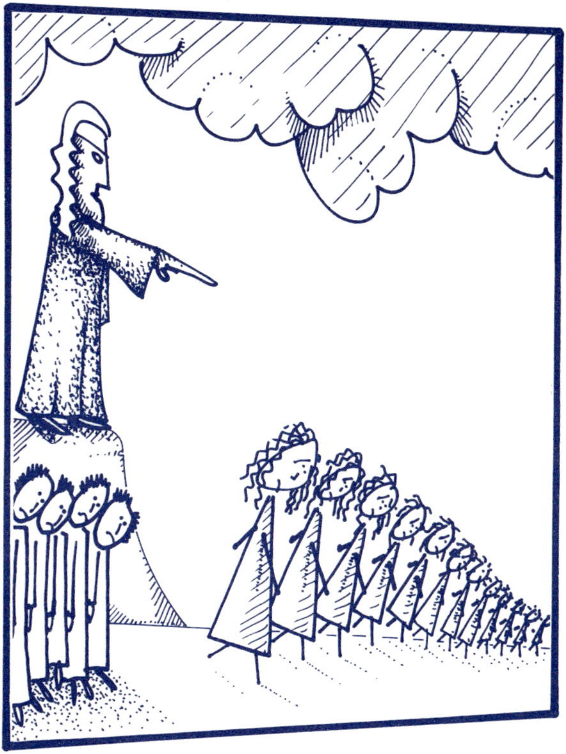

O is for OREB,
a captain of Midian.
They delivered his head
to a "hero" named Gideon.

See Judg 7:25

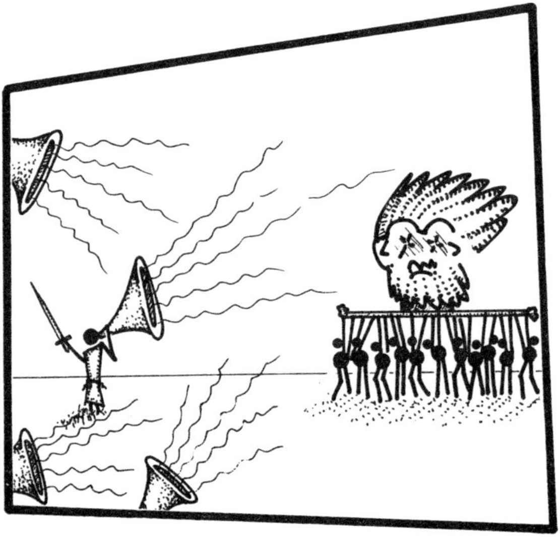

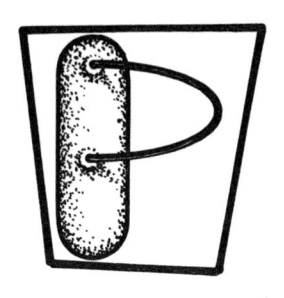

P is for PHOEBE,
who labored with Paul.
This deaconess proved
women can have a call.

See Rom 16:1

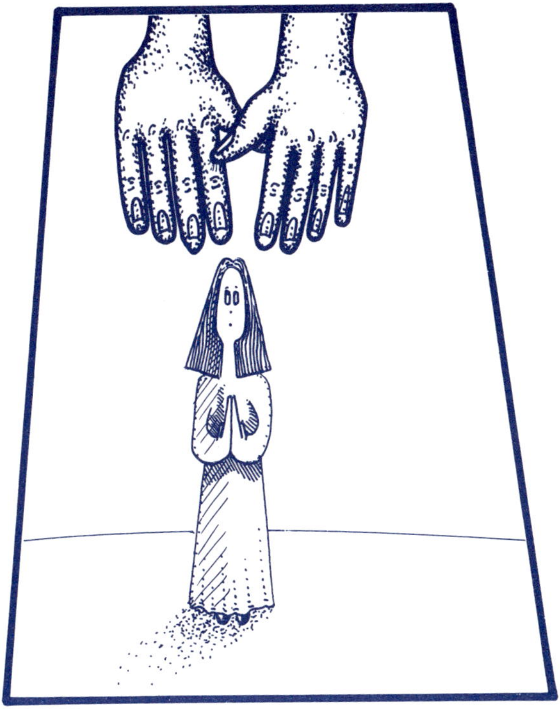

Q is for QUELLE,
the *source* always cited.
Lucky for Mark
it was not copyrighted.

See Mt; Mk; Lk

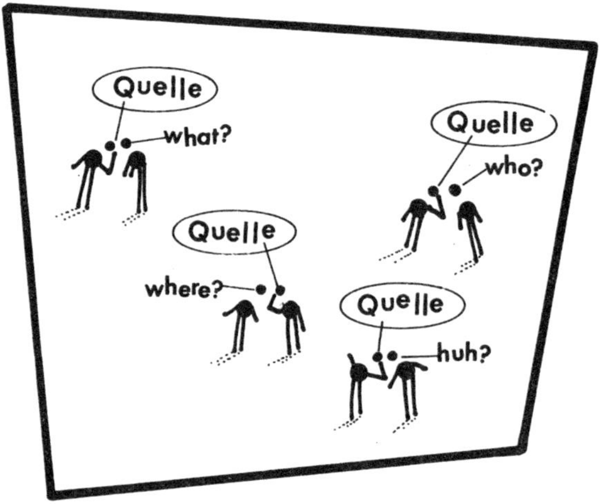
Quelle
what?
Quelle
who?
Quelle
where?
Quelle
huh?

R is for REBEKAH,
 made one son cheat another.
It is wise to stay on
the good side of your mother.

See Gen 25:27-34, 27:1-40

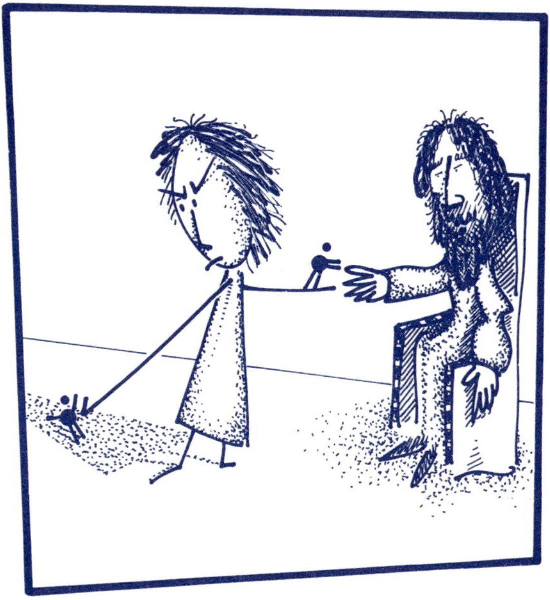

S is for SAUL,
driven out of his mind
when his popular ratings
were lagging behind.

See 1 Sam 18-31

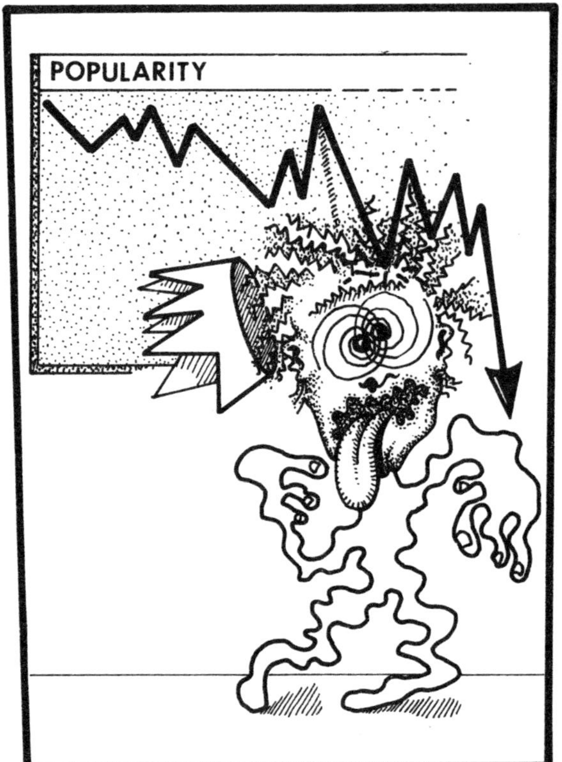
POPULARITY

T is for TITUS,
who caused some division
by resisting a plan
for enforced circumcision.

See Gal 2

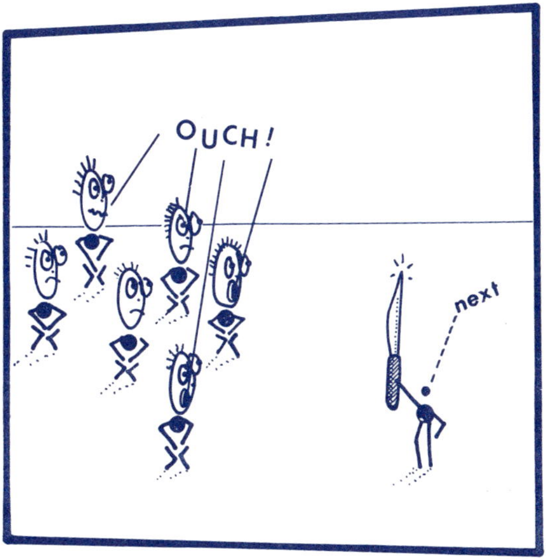
OUCH!
next

U is for URIAH,
   forced to give up his life
while a king took his widow
to bed and to wife.

See 2 Sam 11

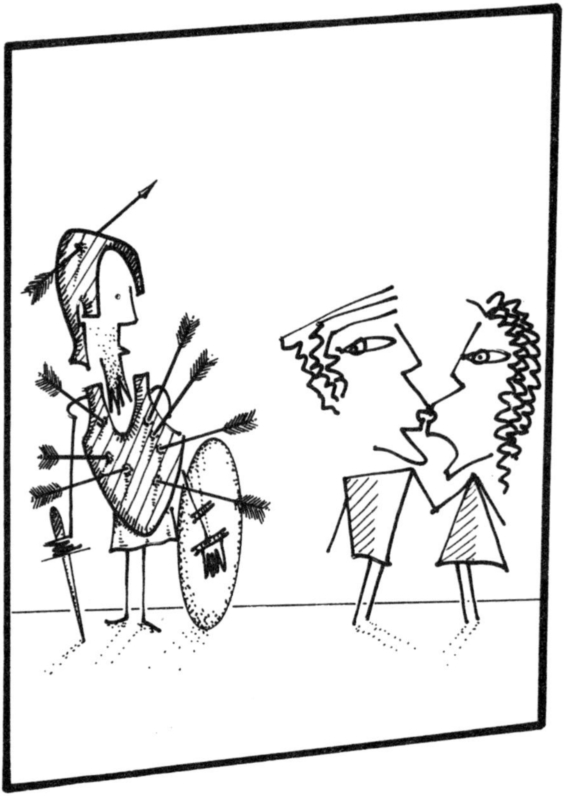

V is the VATICAN
   Scriptures don't mention.
So why do we now
pay it so much attention?

See Mt 16:18

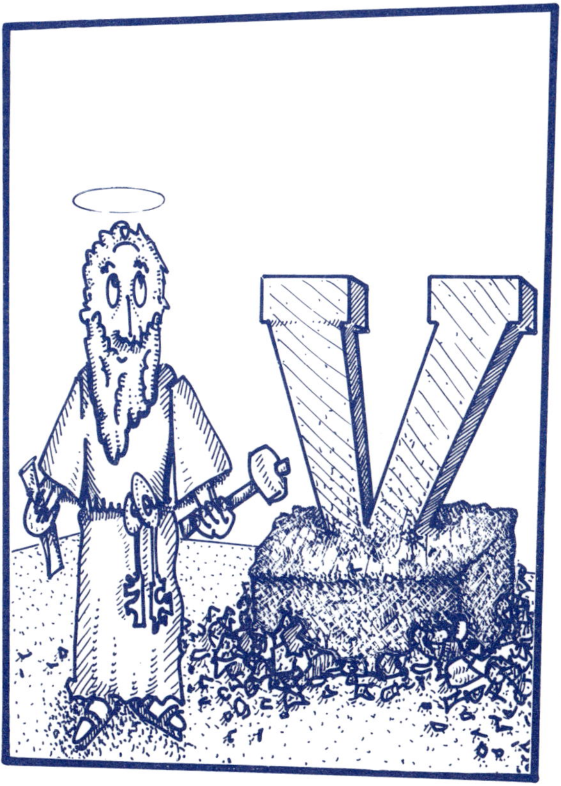

W is for WOMEN
whose names are forgotten,
except in the lines
that begin with begotten.

See Gen 36:1-39; Mt 1:1-17

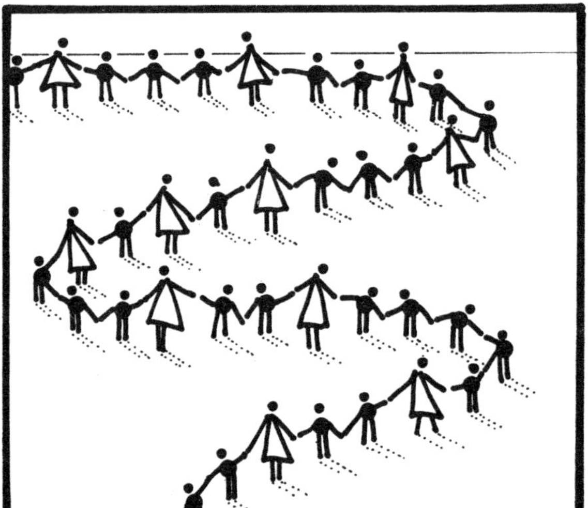

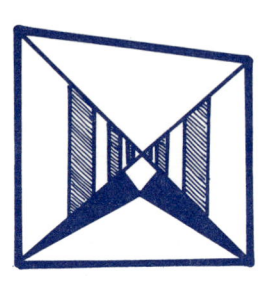

X is for XERXES,
the great Persian king,
the only "two-x"er
who did anything.

> *See Ezra 4:6; Dan 9:1*
> *(Also called* Ahasuerus*)*

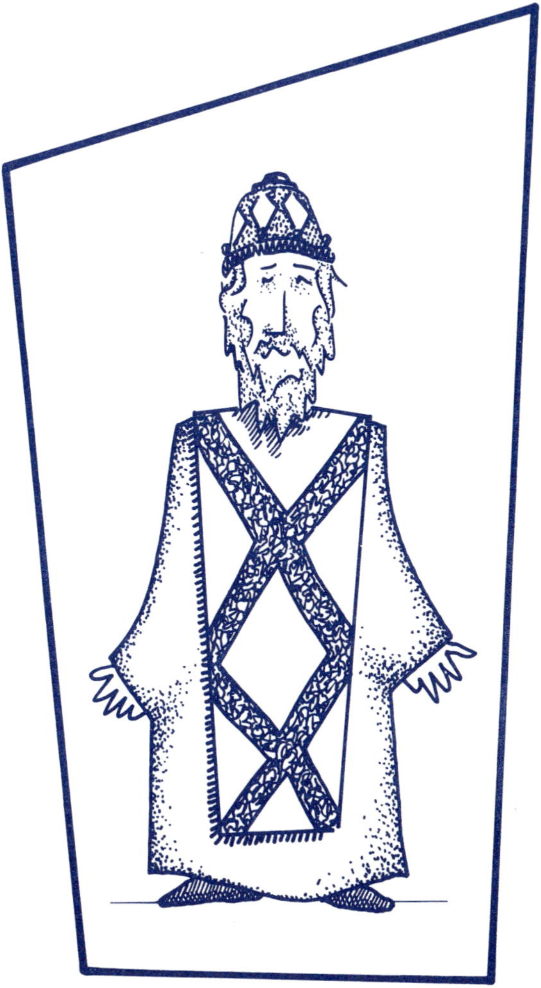

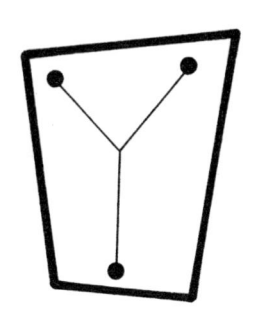

Y is for YAHWEH,
whose name is not said.
Then why say we "he"
and not "she" instead?

See Ex 3:13-14, 6:2-3

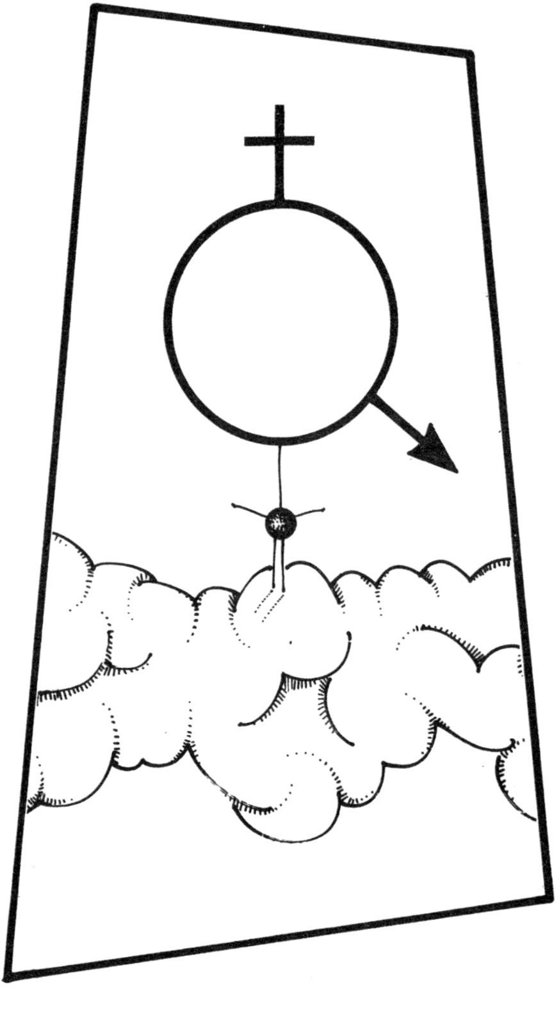

Z is for ZACHARY,
   struck dumb in one stroke,
because he considered
God's word as a joke.

See Lk 1:5-80.

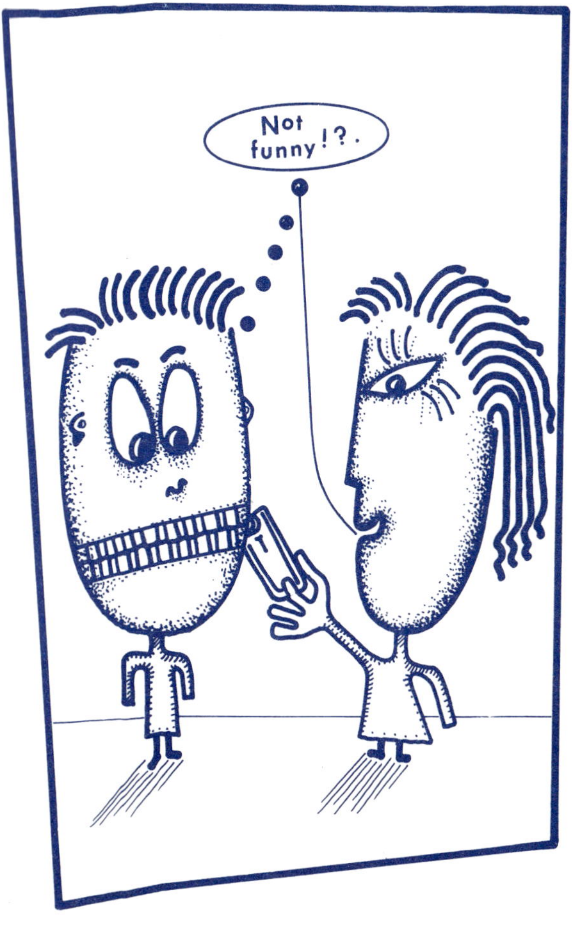
Not funny!?.

About the Humorists

Helen Reichert Lambin is the co-author of *Questions of Christians*, a four volume discussion program of the Gospels, published by ACTA Publications. *Volume 3: Matthew's Response* has been chosen as one of the top fifteen Bible study programs in the book *Picking the "Right" Bible Study Program* by Sr. Macrinca Scott, OSF (ACTA Publications, 1992).

ISZ is the pen name of the artist Richard Struben of Chicago. He has had several one person shows and is represented by several galleries around the country.

Rev. William Burke is a priest of the Archdiocese of Chicago. He is the author of *'Shua*, a fictional account of the life of Jesus as seen through the eyes of a childhood friend, which is published as a book, audio and video tape by ACTA Publications. Fr. Burke can also be heard with Fr. Don Cunningham on the classic comedy audio tape *Veil of Veronica*, as well as on the audio tape *Imagination in Preaching*, also available from ACTA Publications.

All ACTA Publications products are available from your local Christian bookseller or by calling 800-397-2282.